Original title:
The Whispering Fern

Copyright © 2025 Creative Arts Management OÜ
All rights reserved.

Author: Sophia Kingsley
ISBN HARDBACK: 978-1-80581-709-3
ISBN PAPERBACK: 978-1-80581-236-4
ISBN EBOOK: 978-1-80581-709-3

Shadows of the Ancient Grove

In the grove where shadows dance,
A squirrel steals a hazel glance.
He tripped on roots, what a sight,
As birds laugh on with pure delight.

Mossy jokes float in the air,
Where trees gossip without a care.
Frogs croak in a silly tune,
While fireflies party under the moon.

Whispers of the Hidden Glade

A raccoon rummages for a snack,
Found a hat, he wears it back!
The owls hoot, 'What a silly thing!'
As crickets join and start to sing.

The ferns giggle, tickled by breeze,
Nature's humor flows with ease.
Laughter echoes through the trees,
In melodies that sway with glee.

Tales from the Leafy Depths

Beneath the leaves, a secret hide,
Where mushrooms party, side by side.
A timid mouse with a cheese delight,
Wobbles and tumbles, oh what a sight!

The tall ferns wave to all who pass,
As laughter spreads like dew on grass.
A butterfly tells a joke so grand,
That even daisies can't help but stand.

Voices in the Shimmering Shade

The shady nook is quite the scene,
Where chattering leaves are always keen.
Bugs wearing hats dance with a twist,
While the sunbeams do their silly mist.

A gnome with a grin shares a tale,
Of fish that walk and a snail that sails.
A frog joins in, and with a jump,
He lands right on a mushroom's hump.

Tales Etched in Green

In a wood where secrets grow,
Frogs in tuxedos steal the show.
They croak out jokes on leafy seats,
While squirrels debate their fashion feats.

A rabbit dons a sunhat wide,
Claiming it's a style with pride.
Turtles dance, though slow and sly,
In this realm where giggles fly.

Serenity under the Canopy's Shade

Beneath the leaves, where laughter's loud,
A moose can waltz and feel so proud.
The owls with spectacles now read,
As chipmunks plan their acorn feed.

The wind tells tales of things absurd,
A parrot's jokes, quite often blurred.
They chuckle 'neath the arching boughs,
Where even moles wear party crowns.

Beneath the Fractal Currents of Life

In pattern's art, the bugs parade,
Debating if it's cool to fade.
A butterfly, with colors bright,
Decorates the dance floor right.

A beetle dons a shiny cap,
While crickets sing a lilting rap.
Here wisdom's found in leaf and wind,
Where laughter's play can never end.

Gentle Sighs of the Arboreal

Under branches, laughter rings,
As hedgehogs try to learn some swings.
A worm complains that's far too high,
But blossoms near say, "Give it a try!"

An artful hummingbird drops by,
To paint a scene before your eye.
And when the sunset lights the glade,
The forest winks, invitations laid.

Tales from the Verdant Veil

In the shady grove, plants jest,
A mushroom wears a little vest.
The daisies dance in silly lines,
While ants paraded, sipping pines.

A squirrel tries a funny leap,
But trips and lands in leafy heap.
The crickets croon a cheeky tune,
While thorns just chuckle, 'What a boon!'

The breeze joins in, with ticklish flair,
Brushing past a chubby hare.
It giggles soft as acorns fall,
Creating laughter, one and all.

Underneath tall ferns they roam,
Each critter claims a leafy home.
In playful brawl, they twist and twirl,
In this green world, come give a whirl!

Secrets of the Leafy Silence

A snail named Steve, quite the trickster,
Claims he can run—oh, what a twister!
He puffs and puffs, but then he flops,
As leaves and laughter form the stops.

The foxes hide in leafy hues,
Playing peekaboo in their shoes.
With each rustle, giggles spread,
As mushrooms giggle, 'Time for bed!'

The branches sway, a funny tune,
Trees shake hands beneath the moon.
With whispers soft as morning dew,
They share the jokes that only few knew!

Yet every time they share a laugh,
A wobbly owl shows off a gaffe.
He fluffs his feathers, strikes a pose,
And tumbles down, right on his toes!

Echoes Beneath the Canopy

Beneath the leaves, a tale unfolds,
Of silly toads and frogs so bold.
With splashes grand, they dance and dive,
Like clowns of water, oh so alive!

A beetle brags of strength and might,
But trips on roots, what a funny sight!
His friends all laugh, they roll and giggle,
As he complains, 'I swear, it's friggled!'

The breeze brings chats from friends afar,
A lizard plays the guitar.
With every strum, the trees all sway,
And sing along, with joy at play!

Then comes the crow, with a caw so loud,
Spreading stories to a gathered crowd.
With every tale, it quacks and quips,
In the garden of giggles, humor sips!

Whispers in the Woodland Breath

While wandering branches softly sway,
The vines conspire in a teasing play.
A hedgehog winks, with prickly style,
As butterflies join in with a smile.

A raccoon juggles berries bright,
But loses one, what a wild flight!
It rolls and tumbles, splashes mud,
A messy act, they all just flood!

From tulips tall, a chorus rings,
Of chirps and cheeps, oh, the joy it brings.
The whimsy dances on a breeze,
In a world where laughter never flees!

So gather round, ye leafy friends,
For tales of joy, that never ends.
In nature's realm, where giggles roam,
Every whisper weaves you home!

Muffled Melodies of Nature

In the woods, where giggles hide,
The leaves are tickled, just inside.
A squirrel dances with grace and flair,
While mushrooms chuckle, needing air.

The brook gurgles jokes, oh so sly,
As crickets chirp, they can't deny.
A rusty nail gives a little wink,
And trees just sway, too shy to think.

Frogs croak loudly, claiming their throne,
While ants wear crowns made of sweet cone.
Each rustle adds to playful beats,
As nature's laughter forms the treats.

The sun peeks in with a childish grin,
Inviting all in a game to win.
In this forest full of jesters' song,
Where giggles bloom, we all belong.

Beneath the Canopy's Embrace

Beneath the leaves, a party brews,
With whispers soft, and silly cues.
A raccoon juggles acorns with pride,
As a butterfly flutters, its colors wide.

Bamboo bends, making big eyes,
While shadows hide their teasing spies.
The ants march now in silly stance,
Giving the rocks a well-timed dance.

A woodpecker shows off its best moves,
While moles plot pranks, creating grooves.
Laughter erupts in the bright moon's light,
As night creatures bring joy to the night.

The trees giggle, swaying with glee,
As fireflies glow like confetti.
With nature's humor, not a care in sight,
Together we laugh under the starlit night.

Hidden Echoes of Earth

In the soil, secrets twist and twirl,
A dance of roots, a fun little whirl.
Worms whisper sweet nothings around,
While dandelions giggle without sound.

Pebbles gossip as they roll and rock,
Grinning at leaves like a happy flock.
Underfoot, the ants plan their spree,
Each little critter a friend to be.

Caterpillars munch with silly style,
As sunbeams shine, they bask for a while.
The echoes of laughter linger near,
Creating a symphony for all to hear.

Now shadows stretch, claiming their play,
With whispers and chuckles, they dance away.
The earth lays quiet, a smile in its vein,
For nature's joy, is never in vain.

The Silent Language of Leaves

Leaves rustle softly, sharing a jest,
In a world where giggles never rest.
A breeze slips through with a ticklish touch,
Causing the trees to giggle so much.

Branches wiggle, playing peek-a-boo,
While clouds drift by, sharing laughs too.
Acorns clap like they know the beat,
Turning the forest into a grand treat.

The moss hums quiet, just like a spy,
Holding secrets no one can deny.
And as the sunlight dances along,
Every leaf chimes in a merry song.

Swinging leaves, with their chatter and cheer,
Crafting a world that's fun and clear.
In every shimmer, laughter takes flight,
Nature's whispers, a pure delight.

The Lush Enigma

In the shadows of the frond, they dance,
With leafy hats and a jolly prance.
One giggles while the others sigh,
Underneath the curious sky.

A squirrel joins, thinks he's a star,
Chasing ferns near and far.
He slips, he flips, on his fuzzy tail,
Leaves the others to laugh without fail.

The breeze carries secrets often told,
By these plants, both shy and bold.
They whisper jokes in leafy tones,
While playing tag with gnarled stones.

At twilight's glow, the fun's in full
With ferns that sing and squirrels that pull.
A wild waltz in the garden green,
Where plants have rib-tickling routines.

Rustling Secrets of the Green Isle

Amidst the greens, a jest takes flight,
A daisy giggles with all its might.
The ferns are gossiping 'bout the rain,
While crickets add beats, like a train.

A wandering snail shows off his shell,
Claims it's a condo, oh boy, so swell!
The ferns all blush, they roll their eyes,
Saying, "That guy is full of lies!"

They chatter on about the sun,
While ants hustle - oh, what fun!
Sneaky shadows skip and hop,
As laughter rises, it just won't stop.

The moon peeks in, takes a look,
In their world, there's a funny book.
Where leaves can chuckle, roots can tease,
And nature thrives with playful ease.

Echoed Lives Among the Spheres

In a glen where shadows play,
Ferns gather for a sunny day.
Whispers bounce from leaf to leaf,
Sharing tales beyond belief.

A dandelion claims he's tough,
Flexing petals, feeling buff.
But the ferns just roll their green eyes,
For he's puffed up, small in size!

Fruit flies spread rumors, oh so bold,
Of secret dance-offs, yet untold.
Branches sway in laughter shared,
While the shyer buds feel impaired.

As twilight drapes the scene with light,
The ferns hold court, all feeling bright.
Together they hum a merry tune,
In a jest filled ballroom, beneath the moon.

A Tapestry of Verdant Secrets

On a sunny porch, ferns spin tales,
Of their adventures beyond the trails.
One claims she's danced with a butterfly,
While others cheer and tease nearby.

A chap who's mossy brags again,
"I once snuck wine from a sleeping hen!"
The ferns burst into laughter loud,
Creating mirth among the crowd.

The breeze curls in to hear the fun,
Filling the air, oh, so undone.
With roots that wiggle, and fronds that sway,
Their laughter makes the world feel gay.

As dusk creeps in with sleepy sighs,
They wrap their secrets 'neath the skies.
Where plants can giggle, and life's a jest,
In verdant realms, they thrive the best.

Whispers Beneath the Twilight Canopy

In the dusk, leaves giggle low,
Tickled by breezes that gently blow.
Sassy vines dance with quirky glee,
Chasing each other like silly bees.

Mossy cushions hold secrets tight,
While critters plan their midnight flight.
A squirrel snickers, full of mischief,
As shadows blend like a car's backfirth.

Frogs croak tunes that sound absurd,
Competing with crickets, so often heard.
A badger hums, thinks he's in a band,
While the night slips on, all leafy and grand.

Laughter echoes beneath the trees,
Whispers of nature's funny decrees.
Tomorrow they'll do it all over again,
In the twilight realm where the giggles begin.

Soliloquies in the Fern-touched Shade

Amidst the fronds, a wise old tree,
Claims he's the grand sage of the spree.
With leaves as pages, he pens his lore,
Though squirrels chip in with their own rapport.

The worms discuss the best kinds of dirt,
While beetles burrow, their helmets alert.
Each tale spun has a twisty end,
As shadows snicker, the daylight bends.

A grasshopper's joke cracks the still of noon,
He leaps with laughter, like a silly cartoon.
The moss rolls its eyes, not buying the hype,
As laughter drips like dew off a ripe.

With every quip, the ferns all sway,
In nature's ballet, where they laugh and play.
Under the shade, life's chuckles collide,
In a leaf-laden world where dreams abide.

A Voyage in the Silken Dapple

Beneath the sun, silk threads entwine,
Spiders weave tales, oh so divine.
A ladybug shrugs, 'What's the fuss?'
While grass blades whisper, 'Come ride the bus!'

Fireflies blink with mischief in tow,
Lighting up jokes that come and go.
Caterpillars chuckle, 'We're not quite through!'
As they munch their way through the morning dew.

A dragonfly shouts, 'Join the parade!
With wings of magic, we'll never fade!'
With every flap, the humor grows,
In this dappled world where laughter flows.

When dusk drops down like a gentle sigh,
Silken shadows dance, oh me, oh my!
A voyage of whimsy beneath the sky,
With giggles of nature, just passing by.

Echoing Dreams in Leafy Solitude

In leafy corners, dreams take flight,
Where whispers play in the hush of night.
Chubby bunnies, with ears so wide,
Hiding their tales they can't abide.

A fox prances, claiming he's tall,
While all the while, he's hardly at all.
Ambitions grand, but with a twist,
As the shadows giggle at the humor missed.

Dancing daisies join in the joke,
With petals spinning, a fragrant cloak.
They soapbox talk on growth and bloom,
While worms lament in their earthy gloom.

Through the rustling leaves, laughter drips,
As every heartbeat echoes in quips.
In the twilight hush, dreams slide like fire,
In the solitude of whispers, we conspire.

The Language of Green Shadows

In a meadow bright with green,
The plants hold secrets, oh so keen.
They giggle and wiggle, quite absurd,
Speaking softly without a word.

The daisies wink, the grasses sway,
Chatting gossip in their own way.
"Who knew that ferns could dance so spry?"
As leaves rustle, they slyly sigh.

Beneath the fronds, a party brews,
With bumblebees in fancy shoes.
A toad joins in, quite out of tune,
His croak stands out, a funny boon.

So listen close, in peace you'll find,
A humor that leaves all gloom behind.
In shadows green, the laughter's found,
A woodland world spinning round and round.

Serenade of the Shaded Realm

In twilight's glow, the shadows play,
Leaves hum sweet tunes in a cheeky way.
A squirrel finds a nutty joke,
As branches sway, we might all choke!

The rabbits joke, they hop and tease,
Claiming that grass can dance with ease.
Frogs join in on a bouncing spree,
Each croak a line of comedy!

A snail slips past, with rhythmic giggle,
He thinks he's fast, but he's so little.
The ferns bow low, with leafy cheer,
Swaying and laughing, they bring near.

What fun it is in shades so bold,
With whispers of stories yet untold.
Each rustle hints at laughter's call,
In this green realm where we stand tall!

Soft Echoes of Nature's Heart

The leaves gossip like silly friends,
In nature's club where laughter bends.
A leaf drops down, with a whoosh and swirl,
Declaring, "I'm the best in this world!"

Mushrooms giggle, all dressed in spots,
Claiming that they hold the best thoughts.
A breeze teases, rustles the grass,
"Did you hear that? Oh, do let it pass!"

Caterpillars take up the dance,
Twisting their bodies, oh what a chance!
With each little wiggle, they aim to impress,
While ants march by, thinking it's a mess.

So hear the echoes where laughter reigns,
In soft whispers, joy never wanes.
Nature's heart beats with playful glee,
In this laughing world, oh, just let it be!

Conversations in the Mossy Realm

Between the stones, a dialogue flows,
Where mossy friends share all that they know.
A snail with style bounds down a rock,
Saying, "Slow and steady is my clock!"

Lichen laughs while fondly recalling,
How last week's rain had them all sprawling.
"Who knew we'd grow such a fine green mat?"
They joke about the birds and that cat!

A beetle rolls by, with a grand old tale,
"Last night's dessert was quite a fail!
I tried a twig, thought it'd be sweet,
But ended up stuck on someone's feet!"

So here in this realm, where moss holds sway,
The chatter of life just makes our day.
In green corners, where laughter's bright,
Let's stay and enjoy this merry night!

Secret Lives of the Garden Shade

In the nook where shadows play,
A snail practices ballet.
The worms wear tiny hats all day,
And dance while slugs just sway.

The mushrooms hold a party grand,
With whispers shared across the land.
The carrots form a rock band,
With radishes taking a stand.

The bees throw jokes like confetti,
While flowers twirl, getting sweaty.
A garden gnome starts feeling petty,
Because his dance moves aren't ready.

Toadstools giggle behind the trees,
As daisies sway in the breeze.
Each plant conspires with great ease,
To make the garden's laughter freeze.

Soft Echoes in the Twalks

Down the twists where critters creep,
A hedgehog snores, he's lost in sleep.
A rabbit's joke makes mice all leap,
  While ants are planning a food heap.

The brook hums tunes of old-time lore,
While frogs a-prank, the flies they score.
A snail bets high, 'I won't move more!'
  While crickets laugh upon the floor.

Leaves chatter softly, secrets spread,
Squirrels wear wigs upon their heads.
  An acorn wishes it were bread,
Dreaming of toast, it's quite widespread.

At dusk, the shadows play and tease,
The twalks hum like a gentle breeze.
A firefly's lights give all a freeze,
  As they tease the stars from trees.

Ferny Vigil by the Stream

Beside the stream where ferns converse,
A frog pretends he's quite diverse.
He speaks in rhymes, oh what a curse,
While fish giggle, it's quite the verse.

The bubbles pop like laughter shared,
As water sprites announce they're scared.
They play hide and seek, quite unprepared,
While dragonflies act quite ensnared.

The stones are teachers, wise and old,
With stories of both brave and bold.
And each new tale must be retold,
While moss hoards secrets, green and gold.

In this lively stream, humor streams,
Where ferns watch over all our dreams.
The night is filled with soft moonbeams,
As laughter dances through the gleams.

Tales Woven in the Woodland Weaves

In the woodland where the critters meet,
A squirrel juggles acorns neat.
The raccoon stands up on his feet,
A dance-off starts, what a treat!

The trees sway low, their branches play,
With whispers from the night and day.
While hedgehogs tell tales, come what may,
Of a snail who dreams to fly away.

A wise old owl, with specs he wears,
Reads jokes from leaves, and everyone stares.
The rabbits snicker, it's all in pairs,
While passing foxes throw up their glares.

Beneath the stars, where misfits roam,
Giggling spirits find their home.
In nature's fun, we all are known,
Woven tales of joy have grown.

Breaths of the Woodland

In the woods, a leafy dance,
Squirrels prance in silly chance.
Frogs wear hats, they croak and leap,
While rabbits giggle, wake from sleep.

Breezes tickle leafy greens,
Sprightly moss shares nutty scenes.
Woodpeckers drum a jolly tune,
As owls bob heads, night's buffoon.

Gnomes on stilts, they roam about,
Chasing shadows, squealing shout.
Even trees, they sway with glee,
As critters toast with nutty tea.

Each twist and turn, a laugh to find,
With every rustle, joy entwined.
In these woods, the fun's not strained,
Where every breath, a joke is gained.

Enigmas of the Ferny Realm

In the realm where ferns do giggle,
Mice in tophats dance and wriggle.
Snakes in bow ties do a slide,
While ladybugs take joyrides wide.

Frogs play poker 'neath a bush,
Betting flies in a wild rush.
Each paw's a card, each wing a bet,
Silly games we won't forget.

Bouncy mushrooms joke and tease,
Giving all the critters ease.
With laughter echoing 'round the glen,
Even the stones are laughing, then.

So wander here and take a chance,
Join the woodland's funny dance.
In the ferns, giggles take their flight,
Making every day feel bright.

Soft Secrets of the Sylvan Shade

In soft shade where whispers bloom,
Bunnies boast, dispelling gloom.
Ferns exchange their slyest jokes,
While woodchucks crack up, rolling oaks.

Breezes gossip through the leaves,
Telling tales of trickster thieves.
Who stole the acorn? Who took flight?
Blame it on the raccoons' bite!

Under branches, laughter plights,
Where fairies peek and share their sights.
Elves on mushrooms sip their brew,
As sunbeams dance on morning dew.

In the shade, each giggle's sweet,
With tales of mishaps, sure to greet.
Come, my friend, and join the play,
In soft secrets, let's laugh away.

The Untold Stories of the Woodland Floor

Beneath the trees, mischief brews,
Where snails wear glasses, share the news.
Ants on roller-skates do race,
While daisies grin, their best face.

Twirling foxes in a line,
Chasing shadows, oh! So fine.
Every twig a microphone,
To tell each tale of what's been sown.

Crickets' songs take funny turns,
While sunlight spills like smooth concerns.
Little creatures gather 'round,
In their tales, pure joy is found.

So wander through this tale of glee,
Where every spot hides laughter free.
In the woods, where stories soar,
Every whisper opens a door.

Murmurs of Forgotten Roots

In the garden, secrets spin,
Beneath the soil, a playful grin.
Worms do the tango, plants in a trance,
Roots whisper jokes, a leafy romance.

Raccoons roll dice, nature's own game,
Squirrels debate who's wild and tame.
With every rustle, a giggle is heard,
Life's little quirks, like a bent-up bird.

The ivy winks with a leafy jest,
While daisies play poker, who's the best?
Stones sit grumpy, mossy and green,
In the chatter of roots, oh what a scene!

Sunbeams chuckle, shadows conspire,
In this wild comedy, we all retire.
Laughter in leaves, a humorous blend,
With the garden as stage, the fun never ends.

The Quiet Harmony of Nature's Bounty

Beneath a sprout, the raccoon yells,
"Who stole my berries?"—it's full of spells.
The caterpillar giggles, hiding on a rung,
In the world of greens, happy tunes are sung.

The tomatoes chat with the curious peas,
As the corn whispers secrets to the bees.
"A cucumber's too cool!" every vine does shout,
While the broccoli bows, never in doubt.

On the swing of branches, a breeze makes fun,
The sun's bright chuckle makes the day run.
Nature's delight, in costumes of green,
Where laughter thrives, and joy is seen.

With bees drumming softly, a band plays on,
A toad croaks a tune at the break of dawn.
In this playful show, all worries float,
It's a nature's ode, as laughter takes note.

Haunting Melodies of Downy Leaves

In the moon's glow, the leaves do sway,
Their whispers hint at a fright-filled play.
Ghosts of the garden twirl and prance,
With shadows that giggle in a leafy dance.

The owls throw parties, with bats in tow,
"Who's the best dancer?" as branches bow low.
Underneath starry lights, creatures all meet,
In this haunted bash, they laugh on repeat.

Laughter erupts, the bushes delight,
While the crickets strum tunes deep into the night.
A spider spins yarns, weaving wild tales,
As the moonlight chuckles, rippling the trails.

In this spooky garden, where laughter is found,
The leaves share jokes, a ghostly sound.
Among shadows and glimmers, life's antics unfold,
With a spectral tune that's joyful and bold.

The Veil of Verdure's Secrets

Behind the green veil, secrets abound,
A squirrel with plans that astound.
With acorns galore, it plots a spree,
Dancing through branches, so wild and free.

Beneath the ferns, a party is had,
With mushrooms as guests, oh isn't it rad?
The ladybugs gossip, and ants join in,
Playing tag with the breeze, laughter akin.

Ticklish grass blades wiggle with glee,
As the flowers share tales of bumblebee.
The daisies debate who did win the race,
In this vibrant place, no frown leaves a trace.

In nature's embrace, it's a riot of mirth,
With each little creature, celebrating earth.
In the shush of the greens, humor reigns supreme,
A whimsical world, where fun's a dream.

Timelessness in the Fern Clusters

In the green shade, where giggles hide,
The ferns tell tales with a leafy pride.
They twist and dance with a lightly sway,
Whispering secrets of a leafy play.

Laughter bubbles from the hidden glade,
As they gossip 'bout the sun and shade.
"Did you see that bug? It thought it could fly!"
"Oh, please, dear frond, it just made us sigh!"

A squirrel tiptoes, with a twitchy nose,
Stumbling on roots, in a playful pose.
"Don't mind me," says he, with a cheeky grin,
Trying to dance, but falling again!

While petals fall in a merry swirl,
The ferns throw parties with a joyful twirl.
"Join us for fun, it's a forest spree!"
Where shadows laugh and all are free.

The Poesy of Shaded Paths

Under canopies of leafy delight,
The ferns hold up poetry, soft and light.
"Read us a line!" they seem to implore,
As leaf-lined shelves hide laughter galore.

A rabbit in glasses, reading with flair,
Tripping on roots, it's a comical affair.
"Shh! Not too loud, or you'll scare the breeze!"
But chuckles escape, carried with ease.

A ladybug joins, wearing a hat,
In the shade, it's hard to stay flat.
"Did you get my last haiku, dear friend?"
The squirrels replied, "One day, we'll blend!"

As they gather 'round for a verse or two,
The humor flows, like morning dew.
With wink and nod, they weave a jest,
In the shaded paths, there's never rest.

Whims of the Forest Breath

On a starlit night, the ferns come alive,
With whispers of whimsy, nowhere to strive.
They wiggle and jiggle with glee and mirth,
Telling tales of what's hidden beneath earth.

A wise old owl takes a seat on a branch,
"Let's have a party, just give me a chance!"
With twinkling eyes, the ferns all agree,
To dance in the moonlight, wild and free!

They sway to the rhythm of the forest's beat,
With critters all joining, it's quite the feat.
"Watch out for me!" a hedgehog quips loud,
As he rolls in the fronds, proud as a crowd!

So together they frolic, beneath starlight's glow,
In the whimsical night where all laughter flows.
A giggling fern leads, oh what a sight,
In the quirkiest forest, all is delight!

Secrets Beneath the Fern Fronds

Beneath green shadows where mischief does dwell,
 Ferns play their tricks, weaving tales to tell.
"Got a secret? Come share!" they beckon and sway,
 In their leafy kingdom, where giggles hold sway.

A turtle in glasses peeks from his shell,
 "What's the scoop, my friends? Do tell, do tell!"
They whisper and chuckle, sharing delight,
 "Last week a bird tried to sing in the night!"

A parade of ants march in funny lines,
 With tiny trumpets and rhythms that shine.
"Step aside, ladies! We're on a quest!"
 While the ferns just snicker, enjoying their jest.

The sun dips low, and the moon starts to gleam,
 As the ferns weave secrets, like a wild dream.
With a flick of a frond, they signal goodnight,
 In the realm of the ferns, everything's bright!

Fragrant Memories of the Wild

Amidst the fronds there's a smell,
Of sun-kissed dirt and stories to tell.
A creature sneezes, then runs away,
It's a hilarious scene in broad light of day.

Squirrels dance on branches so tight,
Their acorn stash a ridiculous sight.
Laughter echoes where shadows play,
Nature has jokes in its own funny way.

A rabbit hops, its ears out wide,
Trips over roots, oh the critter's pride!
It spins around, half-dazed in glee,
Stumbling through laughter, wild and free.

Even the breeze has a chuckle or two,
Tickling the leaves, giving them a hue.
In the wild, the joy just won't yield,
Fragrant memories in the open field.

Spirits of the Ferny Dell

In the cool dell, where spirits tease,
Laughter spills from the rustling leaves.
Ghosts of ferns hold a lively powwow,
They're all dressed in green, taking a bow.

A tussle erupts, a playful fright,
A sprite in the shadows, ready to bite.
But with a giggle, it takes to flight,
Sprinkling mischief from day till night.

Mushrooms wiggle, as if they rhyme,
To the silly songs of olden times.
Every step finds a giggling gasp,
Nature's sense of humor—who can clasp?

Ferns in formations, a side-splitting sight,
Ready to burst, outta the twilight.
In the dell with spirits who deeply dwell,
Each moment is laughter, a magical spell.

Gentle Hush of the Green Realm

In the green realm where whispers dwell,
A bug spins tales that no one can quell.
With tittering wings the stories unfold,
They seek out sunbeams with hearts bold.

Tiny toadstools join in the act,
Sharing their glee with a hidden pact.
Mushrooms chuckle, they're silly and round,
Gossiping softly without a sound.

Leaves smirk and sway in the dappled light,
Rooted in fun, what a comical sight!
Fluffy clouds giggle close overhead,
As laughter resounds where the wanderers tread.

With every rustle, the jokes abound,
Nature's jesters, forever unbound.
A gentle hush spins a thundering laugh,
In the green realm, you can't help but chaff.

Pulse of the Shaded Wilderness

In shadows deep, the pulse is loud,
With creatures fumbling, oh so proud.
A raccoon slips on a slick, wet stone,
With a belly flop, it's never alone.

The wise old owl looks down with glee,
As the frog leaps up into a tree.
Miscalculating its lofty quest,
Flops back down, which is quite the jest.

Grasshoppers boing with a chirpy cheer,
Their acrobatics create sheer mirth here.
Life's frisky beat in each vibrant hop,
With every jump, the laughter won't stop.

So come explore the wild shades today,
Where humor blooms in the softest way.
The pulse of the wilderness dances and sways,
In nature's embrace, where joy often plays.

Foliage of Forgotten Dreams

In a jungle where jokes grew tall,
A vine tried to tickle a squirrel's call.
It whispered secrets, oh so strange,
While the fern laughed at the forest's range.

Leaves giggled as the breezes played,
With a sly grin, the grass displayed.
"Hey, wait for me!" a log did shout,
As the moss joined in, without a doubt.

A flower bun danced on its stem,
While the ferns belted out a gem.
"Let's all waltz!" cried a boldly sprout,
But they tripped, and that's what it's about!

So we see plants not just to lean,
But ready for fun in a leafy scene.
In a garden where laughter blooms wide,
Even the shy roots wear their pride.

Murmurs Beneath the Fronds

In the underbrush, whispers ignite,
A beetle jigs, giving a fright.
"Who stepped on my toe?" a snail did moan,
While ferns swayed like they'd just been shown.

Fungi got bold and began to roast,
"Who wants a snack?" they cheered as a host.
But a chipmunk nibbled all in sight,
Leaving the crowd in a giggling plight.

The shadows chuckled under the trees,
As the bushes joined in the playful spree.
"Don't tell a soul!" the violets rolled,
As they traded secrets quite uncontrolled.

So life beneath fronds can be quite grand,
With jokes and laughter across the land.
From roots to leaves, a comedic team,
Making the forest a whimsical dream.

Lullabies of the Forest Floor

Softly beneath the boughs they play,
In drowsy tones, the leaves sway.
A snail hummed low, 'tis true, you see,
A lullaby for the busy bee.

A fox crept near, in a curious stance,
Caught in a word of the ferns' prance.
"Did you hear that?" a branch did crack,
"Sounds like a party, and I can't go back!"

The mushrooms formed a tiny band,
With acorn drums, oh wasn't it grand?
Whispers and chuckles in the cool of night,
Every creature tucked in, feeling just right.

So dream with the cracks in the soft moss pie,
With laughter ringing like stars in the sky.
Sleep tight, dear friends, in this leafy delight,
Where funny tales weave under the moonlight.

Veils of Green Serenity

In a haven draped with shades of green,
Laughter erupted, silly and keen.
"Who's tickling me?" a leaf did pout,
As the wind tossed friendships about.

Amidst the ferns, a party tense,
With ivy strings and humor immense.
"Let's sing like frogs!" a nearby sprout,
While the trees chimed in, "There's no doubt!"

A hedgehog joined with a merry grin,
Only to roll and tumble in.
"Help me up!" he squeaked with glee,
As laughter erupted from a nearby tree.

So veil your worries with giggles and cheer,
In this green dress, joy's ever near.
Life's playful dances among all friends,
Let the laughter linger, and never end.

Shadows of the Understory

In the damp shade, a cursor glides,
A squirrel's dance, with nutty pride.
He flips and flops, a comical sight,
Beneath the arms of trees so bright.

Beneath the leaves, where secrets lay,
A toad croaks jokes to the light of day.
With every ribbit, a giggle follows,
As mushrooms nod their heads like swallows.

The roots are gossiping, oh so sly,
"Did you hear the owl? He couldn't fly!"
Laughter ripples through the green community,
As every critter shares their hidden immunity.

In this jungle of fun, all's in good cheer,
Where nature's comedy thrives without fear.
With shadows playing tricks beneath the trees,
Life's a laugh, if you just seize the breeze.

The Silent Grove's Confession

In a grove where silence reigns supreme,
Birch trees gossip, or so it would seem.
"I saw a deer trip over its own hooves,
It spun like a top!"—the laughter proves.

The breezy whispers tickle the air,
While bushes chuckle at antics bare.
A raccoon wearing socks makes quite a chase,
Leaving behind a trail of misplaced grace.

Beneath the ferns, where secrets creep,
The crickets crack jokes while others sleep.
"Did you hear that joke about the lost fawn?
He ran into a tree and his confidence is gone!"

The trees lean in, their barky ears wide,
As mushrooms swirl their caps with pride.
In this silent grove, the laughter flows,
Nature's punchlines only the ferns know.

Murmurs Among the Fronds

Among the fronds, where secrets dwell,
Lies a tale that giggles and swells.
A snail in a hurry, what a sight,
Always late for his slimy night.

A hedgehog's snicker, so sharp and quick,
With spines like armor, he's humor thick.
Prickly remarks fly through the patch,
As laughter cracks, a soft little scratch.

In shadowed corners, the ferns do sway,
Sharing tales of a worm who turned gay.
"I found a flower that danced with the breeze,
Now, I'm the envy of all the bees!"

With each rustled leaf, the whispers cheer,
As critters roll over in mirthful leer.
Among the fronds, the joy is spun,
Laughter echoes, the forest's fun.

Lullabies of the Forest Floor

On the forest floor, a lullaby hums,
As beetles tap dance, with little drums.
Mushrooms sway as they hear the beat,
While ants march proudly on tiny feet.

A rabbit yawns, "Can you keep it down?"
With twinkling eyes but frowning brow.
The badger chimes in, "What's with the noise?
We're trying to sleep, oh silly little boys!"

But crickets call forth with a musical flair,
Flipping their legs without a care.
"Join the party, don't be so shy!
Dance with us under the moonlit sky!"

Beneath the stars, laughter cascades,
As creatures hum tunes in leafy glades.
With every chirp, the night feels warm,
In lullabies of fun, we find our charm.

Resilient Echoes of the Past

In shadows deep, a secret thrives,
Where humor dances, and laughter dives.
Old jokes linger like wisps of air,
Tickling the roots with tender care.

Leaves twirl 'round in a playful spree,
Sharing tales from the olden tree.
With every rustle, there's giggles galore,
Echoing stories, always wanting more.

The past whispers softly, in quirky tones,
As nature chuckles with mischief of stones.
In this joyful realm, history spins,
While the ferns gossip, where fun begins.

So stroll through the woods, with a grin so wide,
Discover delights that nature can't hide.
Each laugh from the leaves, a playful tease,
In echoes of past, let your troubles ease.

Serene Refuge of the Woodlands

Upon a branch, a squirrel struts proud,
Telling tall tales to an invisible crowd.
With acorn props and a flourish of paws,
Each punchline lands like thunderous applause.

Among soft moss, a rabbit hops near,
Cracking up the fungi, letting out cheer.
The trees nod softly, their barks all a-chuckle,
"Who knew a woodland could have such a buckle?"

A snail whispers jokes, slow as can be,
Timing is key; he's the comic decree.
With a grin, he glides, a comedian sly,
Turning a leaf over to catch a dry eye.

In this serene refuge, let laughter erupt,
Nature's giggles are joyfully corrupt.
Woodlands alive with comical jest,
Leave all your worries, let humor invest.

Hushed Conversations with the Green

In the thickets, where giggles abound,
Plants share rumors; who knew they could sound?
Leaves whisper sweet nothings and old witty lore,
Trading wisecracks behind the door.

A wise old tree, with bark worn and gray,
Cracks a joke about a koala's fray.
"Why did he hug? Because branches are free!"
Echoes of laughter spread through the spree.

Breezes carry chuckles, small and discreet,
As dandelions snicker at their own feet.
Petals blush bright with clever retorts,
Even the insects share playful reports.

Hushed conversations between each green friend,
Chatting about mischief, a message to send.
In the silence, a symphony plays,
of giggles and gaffes in nature's good ways.

The Clandestine Realm of Leaves

In the heart of the grove, a secret club thrives,
Where leaves share their quirks, and laughter derives.
With underhanded giggles, they plot their next scheme,
A heist for the sunlight, that's the dream!

The grasses conspire, all huddled like spies,
Swapping tall tales 'neath the brightening skies.
"Did you hear about the worm chasing a bird?"
"Turns out he was just a bit absurd!"

Vines weave around with a comedic twist,
Each detour taken, no plot will be missed.
Fluffy clouds loom as the comedians thrive,
Complaining of shadows, they're keen to arrive.

This clandestine world, full of giggles and cheer,
Where laughter erupts and no one sheds a tear.
So join in the fun in this leafy retreat,
In nature's great playground, the mischief's complete.

Green Conspiracies of Nature

In the verdant hues where shadows creep,
Foliage plots while we are asleep.
With vines that giggle and leaves that tease,
Nature's tricks are sure to please.

The squirrels are scheming, with nuts to stash,
Planning a feast with a bold little dash.
While rabbits hold meetings, oh what a sight,
In the moonlight's glow, they plot through the night.

Whispers abound where soft breezes flow,
As plants exchange secrets, we just don't know.
With humor in roots, they tickle the ground,
A giggle erupts, oh, how it resounds!

The fungi conspire, with whispers of glee,
To lure in the critters for tea and caprice.
Oh, the laughter of leaves, it truly is grand,
In this world of green, it's all well-planned!

The Unseen Dances of the Woodland

Beneath the moonlight, shadows do sway,
Branches twist and turn in a playful ballet.
The mossy carpets, they giggle with glee,
While creatures join in, just wait and see!

A waltz of the weeds, with whispers so spry,
As fireflies buzz by, like stars in the sky.
Each footstep's a rhythm, a song soft and low,
In this revelry deep, where all critters go!

The owls hoot a tune, a raucous refrain,
While raccoons keep time with their paws in the rain.
The laughter resounds in the echoing glade,
While nature's own choir performs unafraid.

So twirl through the night with the roly-poly bugs,
And sway with the trees in their plaid, leafy hugs.
For every leaf rustle and branch that does bend,
Is a wink from the woods, your hilarious friend!

Secrets Linger in the Dampness

In the depths of the wood, where the shadows conspire,
Mushrooms tell tales, sparking laughter and fire.
With damp little whispers, they share their last joke,
As the mist playfully dances around each oak.

The puddles are giggling, reflecting the light,
Inviting the frogs for a splashy delight.
With every croak echoing through the trees,
They start up a chorus, a ribbiting spree!

The ferns hold their breath as the secrets unfold,
In soggy old corners where tales are retold.
And ants in their suits, march to the beat,
Celebrating life from the rain-soaked street.

So step on the moss and feel nature's grin,
In the woodland's embrace, let the laughter begin.
For in every squelch, and the damp of the air,
Lies a memory waiting, for us to share!

Graceful Suspense of the Biome

In the lushness abound, where the leaves intertwine,
A drama unfolds with very little sign.
The fawns tiptoe softly, as if in a show,
While the rabbits hide, with their ears all aglow.

The trees eavesdrop on tales of the day,
While the sunlight flickers, in a rollicking play.
Every rustle's a clue, a mystery to tease,
Beneath the bright boughs, the critters appease.

With whispers of wind, and secrets so grand,
The squirrels are shaking their tiny squirrel hands.
The stories unfold in a twist and a twirl,
In a woodland so spirited, nature's own pearl.

Together they giggle, this curious crew,
In a world where the magic feels vibrant and new.
For laughter is hidden in every small glance,
In the graceful suspense, they all join the dance!

Mystery in the Mossy Nook

In the glade where shadows play,
A squirrel twirls in bright ballet.
Mossy patches, oh so sly,
Tickling toes as critters fly.

The mushrooms giggle, hiding tight,
While bugs break dance in pure delight.
Leaves chatter as they catch the breeze,
Swapping jokes like old-time peas.

Down below, the roots conspire,
To trip the feet of those who tire.
In this nook where sillies dwell,
Nature's secrets giggle well!

Caresses of Sunlight Through Leaves

Sunbeams dance on leafy floors,
While beetles ponder grand old scores.
The rays play peekaboo with the bugs,
As ants give high-fives, huddled in hugs.

Laughter ripples across the glade,
As daisies play a sunny charade.
Grasshoppers prance with airy glee,
A chorus of 'look at me!'

Squirrels trade tales of daring quests,
While dappled light brings out their vests.
In this radiant, leafy show,
Nature's fun never runs low!

Nature's Soft Confidant

The wise old bush whispers low,
Of secrets only critters know.
A rabbit giggles at the frog,
As they share snacks beneath the fog.

Mice and moles hold council tight,
Debating how to dodge the light.
In this chatter, joy runs free,
Sharing wit with agility!

The trees wink with leafy smiles,
While butterflies boast of their miles.
Oh, what a riot this friend can be,
A giggling gang of greenery!

Hidden Harmonies of the Underbrush

Whispers hum where wild things roam,
In thickets that feel like home.
A raccoon juggles shiny finds,
While the hedgehog's clock unwinds.

Crickets chirp a silly tune,
As the fireflies light the moon.
Beneath the leaves, the laughter grows,
With every rustle, joy bestows!

Geckos gossip in the night,
About the stars that shine so bright.
In this underbrush ballet,
Life's a dance in endless play!

The Gentle Laughter of Shadows

In the glade where shadows play,
I saw a squirrel trying ballet.
Mushrooms clapped with tiny glee,
As a rabbit danced with a bee.

The sunbeams giggled, oh so bright,
Tickling leaves in pure delight.
A frog jumped in a wobbly spin,
Chasing laughter with a cheeky grin.

A snail grinned wide, though he was slow,
"Quick! Let's race!" shouted a crow.
But the crow was far too sly,
He flew for fun and waved goodbye.

So, in the shade, we learn with cheer,
That even shadows love to steer.
To laugh and dance amidst the ferns,
Life teaches joy in funny turns.

Enchanted Moments in the Fernery

In the nook where green leaves dwell,
A tiny elf began to yell.
He'd lost his hat, it flew away,
Caught on a breeze that liked to play.

A ladybug, with spots so bright,
Took to the air—what a sight!
She buzzed around, a funny tease,
Daring the flowers to say, "Please!"

Amidst the fronds, a dance began,
With a gnome who wore a silly pan.
His jig was loud but filled with cheer,
Spreading laughter from ear to ear.

So in that fabled, leafy maze,
We find ourselves in childlike craze.
Each moment sparkles with delight,
In a world where joy takes flight.

Dreamscapes Beneath the Canopy

Underneath the leafy roof,
The moonlight danced, with little proof.
A raccoon played his trusty drum,
While crickets strummed a jolly hum.

Dreams floated like the stars above,
As owls hooted tales of love.
A wanderer tripped over a vine,
And the trees shook, "He's doing fine!"

A squirrel sought a midnight snack,
Found a berry, but earned a whack.
With juice now smeared across his face,
He laughed and joined the merry chase.

So whenever you hear whispers mild,
Remember the tricks of nature wild.
From furry friends beneath the sky,
To moments that make you laugh and sigh.

Unfurling Stories from the Earth

Beneath the soil, the secrets stir,
A worm is spinning tales, for sure!
He'll twist and twirl, with such finesse,
While telling tales of a beetle's mess.

A sprightly toad jumped in the mud,
With leaps so wild, he caused a flood.
The ferns took root, and danced around,
In laughter's echo, joy was found.

A clump of moss joined in the song,
Swaying gently, never wrong.
And whispers floated, light as air,
Chasing stories everywhere.

Through roots and leaves, life spins its yarn,
With every turn, a twist, a charm.
In this merry, earthy sphere,
Each tale unfurls with hearty cheer.

www.ingramcontent.com/pod-product-compliance
Lightning Source LLC
Chambersburg PA
CBHW072135070526
44585CB00016B/1694